RosettaStone

Language Learning   Success

D0885188

Workbook

English US	Level 2

English

TRS-WKBK-ENG2-4.0

ISBN 1-883972-82-5

Printed in the United States of America

Fairfield Language Technologies
135 West Market Street
Harrisonburg, Virginia 22801 USA

Telephone: 540-432-6166 or 800-788-0822 in U.S. and Canada
Fax: 540-432-0953
E-mail: info@RosettaStone.com
Web site: www.RosettaStone.com

Worksheet 9-01

I. Fill in the blanks. Two of them have been filled in for you as examples.

__b__ 1. The boys are jumping _____.

__g__ 2. These people are the same gender: _____.

____ 3. Boys and girls are _____.

____ 4. _____ made from the same material.

____ 5. _____ different species.

____ 6. The two pieces of clothing are _____.

____ 7. These people are different genders: _____.

____ 8. These people are the same height: _____.

____ 9. These people are different heights: _____.

____ 10. These flowers are the same color. _____

a. These animals are

b. at the same time

c. different genders

d. made from different materials

e. All of them are red.

f. both of them are five feet tall

g. both of them are female

h. one of them is male, and the other one is female

i. The two shirts are

j. one of them is five feet tall, and the other one is six feet tall

II. Label each picture with a complete sentence. One of them has been labeled for you as an example.

11. __These are the same kind of fish.__ _____

12. _____

13. _____

14. _____

15. _____

16. _____

17. _____

18. _____

19. _____

20. _____

Worksheet 9-02

I. Answer each question with a complete sentence.

Example: Who is that?   **That is Mark.**

1. Who is that?   *that's my son*

2. What's that?   *that is my book*

3. Where is my notebook?   *it's on the desk*

4. Where is my coat?   *here is it*

5. Which way should we go?   *we sould go by this one*

6. Why is he wet?   *he's raining*

7. Why is she in bed?   *becaus she is sick*

8. Why is he screaming?

9. Whose car is this?

10. Which shirt do you like?

II. Fill in each blank with an appropriate question.

Example: What is this?   **This is a dog.**

11. _____   This is a cat.

12. _____   Her name is Susan.

13. _____   Here it is.

14. _____   Because she is sick.

15. _____   That is a bicycle.

16. _____   You should go that way.

17. _____   I'm going for a drive.

18. _____   I want this piece.

19. _____   C A R

20. _____   People go to sleep at eleven o'clock at night.

Asking Questions; Interrogative Pronouns, Adjectives and Adverbs   **ENGLISH**

I. Fill in the blanks.

___ 1. The bus is in the _____ place.

___ 2. This is not the usual length _____.

___ 3. This is _____ for a sheep.

___ 4. This is a common _____.

___ 5. People's faces _____.

___ 6. This is a rare kind _____.

___ 7. This is a _____ stone.

___ 8. This dog is not dressed. _____

___ 9. This dog is dressed. _____

___10. He is wearing _____ the moon.

a. an unusual color

b. That is normal.

c. for a man's hair

d. appropriate clothing for

e. usual

f. means of transportation

g. rare

h. usually look like this

i. of animal

j. That is unusual.

II. Label each picture with a complete sentence.

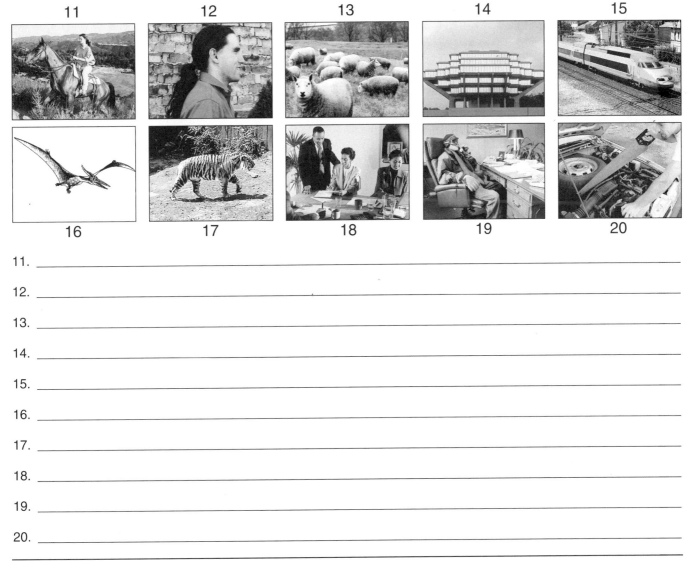

11   12   13   14   15

16   17   18   19   20

11. _____

12. _____

13. _____

14. _____

15. _____

16. _____

17. _____

18. _____

19. _____

20. _____

I. Label each picture with a complete sentence.

1   2   3   4   5

6   7   8   9   10

1. _____

2. _____

3. _____

4. _____

5. _____

6. _____

7. _____

8. _____

9. _____

10. _____

II. Write one sentence as directed.

Examples: Invite Mary Thomson in. Be formal.   Please come in, Mrs. Thomson.

       Ask Susan to get something for you.   Susan, can you reach that for me?

11. Invite Tom Williams in. Be formal.   _____

12. Invite Tom Williams in. Be informal.   _____

13. Ask your mother to reach something for you.   _____

14. Ask your teacher to get something for you.   _____

15. Ask for the pepper.   _____

Forms of Address: Formal and Informal, Singular and Plural   **ENGLISH**

Worksheet 9-05

I. Answer each question with a complete sentence.

1. Are the leaves dead? _____

2. What is the man thinking about? _____

3. What are you thinking about? _____

4. Why is she yawning? _____

II. Circle the singular word.

5. birds
   bird
   apples
   books

6. people
   leaves
   shirt
   feet

7. woman
   women
   girls
   boys

III. Circle the plural word.

8. chair
   dog
   cars
   glass

9. men
   man
   yes
   tree

10. light
    three
    socks
    yellow

IV. Change every singular word into a plural word. Do not forget to change the verbs, too.

> See the **Extra Practice** section at the end of the unit for more practice with plurals.

Example: The man is looking at a book.   <u>**The men are looking at books.**</u> _____

11. The woman is stretching. _____

12. The man is yawning. _____

13. The child is dreaming. _____

14. The boy is speaking. _____

15. The leaf is alive. _____

16. The bird is real, and it is alive. _____

17. The man is reading a book. _____

18. The woman is eating an apple. _____

19. The man is thinking about a math problem. _____

20. The woman is thinking about fishing. _____

ENGLISH   **Alive, Dead, Sleeping, Dreaming, Thinking**

Worksheet 9-06

I. Change every singular word into a plural word. Do not forget to change the verbs, too.

Example: He is wearing a red hat.   <u>They are wearing red hats.</u> _____

1. He is dancing. _____

2. She is not dancing. _____

3. I am wearing a red shirt. _____

4. You are wearing a blue shirt. _____

5. She is giving me a box. _____

6. I am giving him a coat. _____

7. She is giving me the coat. _____

8. You are giving me a green shirt. _____

9. You are taller than I am. _____

10. He is taller than you are. _____

II. Change every plural word into a singular word. Do not forget to change the verbs, too.

Example: They are wearing hats.   <u>She is wearing a hat.</u> _____

11. The boys are dancing. _____

12. They are dancing. _____

13. We are dancing. _____

14. The men are dancing. _____

15. They are reading books. _____

16. The women are giving them coats. _____

17. They are giving the books to the girls. _____

18. The girls are taller than the boys. _____

19. The people are going inside. _____

20. The other people are wearing blue shirts. _____

I. Label each picture with a complete sentence.

1   2   3   4   5

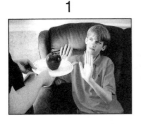    

1. _____

2. _____

3. _____

4. _____

5. _____

II. Circle the positive sentence.

6. This is not an apple.
   This is an apple.
   This is not a house.
   That is not a dog.

7. She does not like carrots.
   He does not want the book.
   I do not need it.
   We like to drink coffee.

III. Circle the negative sentence.

8. That is not red.
   That is blue.
   This is a passport.
   Where are we?

9. You need to buy a car.
   Does he like it?
   She does not want to throw it.
   The ball is white and red.

10. Hello, Mr. Burns.
    Shoes are bigger than cars.
    Be careful!
    Don't touch that!

IV. Change each positive sentence into a negative sentence.

Example: He likes cake.   He does not like cake. _____

11. This is a book. _____

12. This is a passport. _____

13. This is something people need. _____

14. This is something people want. _____

15. She wants the coffee. _____

16. She needs a ladder to reach the window. _____

17. He wants to give her the towel. _____

18. We need help with this. _____

19. Throw me the ball. _____

20. Carry me, please. _____

Worksheet 9-08

I. Fill in the blanks.

___ 1. The man is _____.

___ 2. The woman _____.

___ 3. The boy likes _____.

___ 4. She _____ something.

___ 5. The boy is choosing something _____.

___ 6. There _____ three hats.

___ 7. The boy guesses _____.

___ 8. The boy has _____ fruit to eat.

___ 9. The boy and the girl _____.

___10. He is offering her a glass _____.

a. a choice of

b. from the tray

c. choosing something to eat

d. the candy

e. are

f. doesn't like the dress

g. is offering

h. like each other

i. of soda

j. that the pea is under the black hat

II. Label each picture with a complete sentence.

11. _____

12. _____

13. _____

14. _____

15. _____

16. _____

17. _____

18. _____

19. _____

20. _____

Liking, Choosing, Offering, Guessing   **ENGLISH**

I. Fill in the blanks.

____ 1. She is typing _____.

____ 2. She is putting a _____ into the computer.

____ 3. She answers _____.

____ 4. She hangs _____.

____ 5. Julie _____ a stamp.

____ 6. Julie _____ a folder into the filing cabinet.

____ 7. He is looking up a _____.

____ 8. He is _____ the monitor.

____ 9. He is looking _____ something under the desk.

____10. He is _____ a box shut.

a. is licking

b. taping

c. for

d. on the computer

e. is putting

f. disk

g. looking at

h. the phone

i. up the phone

j. phone number

II. Label each picture with a complete sentence.

11	12	13	14	15

16	17	18	19	20

11. _____

12. _____

13. _____

14. _____

15. _____

16. _____

17. _____

18. _____

19. _____

20. _____

I. Label each picture with a complete sentence.

| 1 | 2 | 3 | 4 | 5 |

1. _____

2. _____

3. _____

4. _____

5. _____

II. Match the words on the left with the contractions on the right.

____ 6. he is   a. isn't

____ 7. cannot   b. doesn't

____ 8. is not   c. he's

____ 9. does not   d. don't

____10. do not   e. can't

III. Change each sentence so that it includes a contraction.

Example: I cannot see.   **I can't see.** _____

11. This woman cannot talk.   _____

12. The man cannot smell.   _____

13. The girl is not helping her friend to stand up.   _____

14. She is helping her friend to stand up.   _____

15. He does not have the key.   _____

16. He is helping her carry the rug.   _____

17. It is here.   _____

18. What is that?   _____

19. Who is that?   _____

20. Do not touch it!   _____

Write the plural form of each word.

1. dress _____
2. box _____
3. bus _____
4. tomato _____
5. bush _____

6. bunch _____
7. baby _____
8. pony _____
9. secretary _____
10. scarf _____

11. knife _____
12. calf _____
13. valley _____
14. roof _____
15. belief _____

16. man _____
17. woman _____
18. child _____
19. ox _____
20. foot _____

21. tooth _____
22. goose _____
23. mouse _____
24. sheep _____
25. fish _____

Crossword Unit 9

Across

2. She is ___ some papers together with a paper clip.
4. This is a ___ color for sheep.
7. I ___ going into a store.
8. Mrs. Smith, are you all ___?
11. This bus is not in the usual ___.
13. She doesn't need the piece of paper; she is putting it into the ___.
15. Are ___ wearing a blue shirt?
17. He is wet because he was in the ___.
20. People eat lunch at ___.
21. People ___ jewelry, but they do not need it.
22. not alive
23. Her ___ is Susie.
24. ___ I take your order, ma'am?

Down

1. These people have different ___ eyes.
3. The man is thinking ___ a book.
5. These are the same kind ___ fish.
6. These flowers are the ___ color.
9. The boy is lifting the chest by ___.
10. The boy ___ that the pea is under the black hat.
12. He is screaming because he is in ___.
14. She is ___ on the computer.
16. People's faces ___ look like this.
17. Mr. Williams, come and look at this, ___.
18. There are two kinds of fruit; the boy has a ___ of fruit to eat.
19. They are jumping ___ the same time.

Worksheet 10-01

I. Fill in the blanks.

___ 1. Jane _____ writing a letter to Lucy.

___ 2. Jane _____ the letter.

___ 3. Jane _____ the letter into the envelope.

___ 4. Jane licks the _____.

___ 5. Jane opens _____.

___ 6. _____ the microwave.

___ 7. _____ the food.

___ 8. _____ the towel.

___ 9. _____ the bathroom.

___10. _____ the food into the microwave.

a. stamp

b. Jane eats

c. Jane goes into

d. puts

e. Jane puts

f. is thinking about

g. folds

h. the mailbox

i. Jane turns on

j. Jane hangs up

II. Using the pictures below, write a story about a person who writes a letter.

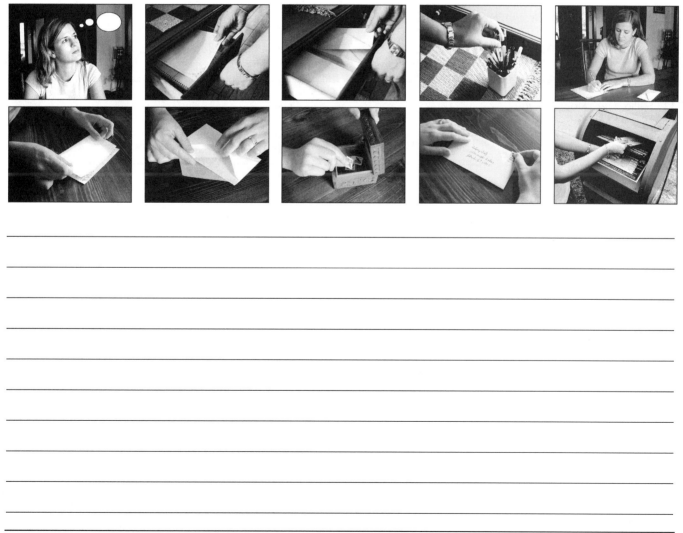

_____

_____

_____

_____

_____

_____

_____

_____

_____

_____

ENGLISH   **Sequential Activities: Writing, Eating and Washing**

I. Fill in each blank with an appropriate question.

1. _____   My address is 486 West Market Street.

2. _____   My telephone number is 555-7891.

3. _____   My birthday is June 28th.

4. _____   My name is Arthur.

5. _____   That's Suzanna.

6. _____   Fine, thank you.

7. _____   Yes, I can help you.

8. _____   I don't know.

9. _____   No, thank you.

10. _____   Yes, please.

II. Write two sentences to finish each conversation.

Example: Hello, Mrs. Brown. How are you?

Fine, thanks. How are you? _____

I'm fine. Today is my birthday. _____

11. Hello, Carl. How are you?

_____

_____

12. What's your address?

_____

_____

13. Excuse me, can you help me?

_____

_____

14. What's your phone number?

_____

_____

15. Who is that over there?

_____

_____

I. Label each picture with a complete sentence.

1 2 3 4 5

6 7 8 9 10

1. _____

2. _____

3. _____

4. _____

5. _____

6. _____

7. _____

8. _____

9. _____

10. _____

II. Answer each question with a complete sentence.

11. What time is the train arriving? _____

12. What time is the train leaving? _____

13. Where can I check my luggage? _____

14. Who could help me carry my luggage? _____

15. Do you have your ticket? _____

16. Are you waiting for the bus? _____

17. Are you on vacation? _____

18. Are you waiting in line to buy a ticket? _____

19. What is the plane doing? _____

20. When you are on vacation, where do you like to go? _____

I. Label each picture with a complete sentence.

1	2	3	4	5

   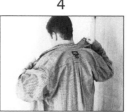 

1. _____

2. _____

3. _____

4. _____

5. _____

II. Fill in the blanks.

_____ 6. Bob _____ a button onto the shirt.   a. is sewing

_____ 7. Bob _____ the shirt into a laundry basket.   b. He is putting

_____ 8. Bob _____ dress clothes that fit.   c. He is matching

_____ 9. _____ the socks.   d. is putting

_____10. _____ the socks into the dryer.   e. is wearing

III. Using the pictures below, write a story about a man who washes his laundry.

_____

_____

_____

_____

_____

_____

_____

Doing the Laundry; Washing, Drying, Folding and Wearing   **ENGLISH**

Worksheet 10-05

I. Write an "A" next to each active sentence and a "P" next to each passive sentence.

Examples:

_P_ The shoe is being thrown by the girl.

_A_ The girl is throwing the shoe.

____ 1. The boy is throwing the ball.

____ 2. The ball is being thrown by the boy.

____ 3. The woman is being kissed by the man.

____ 4. The girl will throw the ball.

____ 5. The boy is tearing the cloth.

____ 6. The ball is being dropped by the boy.

____ 7. The boy's hair has been cut by the woman.

____ 8. The girl's hair will be cut by the woman.

____ 9. The girl has thrown the ball.

____10. The boy will tear the cloth.

II. Change each passive sentence into an active sentence.

Example:

The man's hair is being cut by the woman. — **The woman is cutting the man's hair.**

11. The woman's hair is being combed by the man. _____

12. The plate is being thrown by the boy. _____

13. The boy's hair is being pulled by the girl. _____

14. The ball has been dropped by the boy. _____

15. The ball will be dropped by the boy. _____

III. Change each active sentence into a passive sentence.

Example:

The woman is pulling the girl. — **The girl is being pulled by the woman.**

16. The man is brushing the woman's hair. _____

17. The woman is kissing the man. _____

18. The boy has torn the cloth. _____

19. The man has broken the plate. _____

20. The man will break the plate. _____

I. Fill in the blanks.

___ 1. _____ eating the meal.

___ 2. _____ is eating the meal yet.

___ 3. _____ the dishes into the sink.

___ 4. _____ a sponge to wash the dishes.

___ 5. _____ the dishes.

___ 6. She _____ the milk into the measuring cup.

___ 7. She _____ the milk.

___ 8. _____ are boiling.

___ 9. _____ is eating the potatoes.

___ 10. She is eating _____ .

a. Annette is putting

b. Annette is using

c. She

d. is heating

e. They have finished

f. a snack

g. No one

h. Annette is drying

i. The potatoes

j. is pouring

II. Label each picture with a complete sentence.

11	12	13	14	15

16	17	18	19	20

11. _____

12. _____

13. _____

14. _____

15. _____

16. _____

17. _____

18. _____

19. _____

20. _____

Worksheet 10-07

I. Label each picture with a complete sentence.

| 1 | 2 | 3 | 4 | 5 |

| 6 | 7 | 8 | 9 | 10 |

1. _____
2. _____
3. _____
4. _____
5. _____
6. _____
7. _____
8. _____
9. _____
10. _____

II. Unscramble the words to make a sentence.

Example: is slippers he wearing　　　　<u>He is wearing slippers.</u>

11. is shaving he　　　　_____

12. is she on putting makeup　　　　_____

13. sink the the cleaning boy is　　　　_____

14. someone ironing shirt is a　　　　_____

15. using razor the a is man　　　　_____

16. nightgown she is a wearing　　　　_____

17. is her clipping she fingernails　　　　_____

18. broom she using a is　　　　_____

19. is a to his face wash washcloth using he　　　　_____

20. she putting toothpaste toothbrush on is the　　　　_____

I. Match the words.

____ 1. ruler   a. speed

____ 2. speedometer   b. volume

____ 3. thermometer   c. length

____ 4. scale   d. time

____ 5. clock   e. distance

____ 6. odometer   f. temperature

____ 7. measuring cup   g. weight

II. Cross out the word that does not belong.

Example: boy, girl, man, ~~dragon~~

8. shorter, speed, closer, longer

9. price, weight, long, time

10. miles, hours, pounds, scales

III. Label each picture with a complete sentence.

11.   12.   13.   14.   15.

16.   17.   18.   19.   20.

11. _____

12. _____

13. _____

14. _____

15. _____

16. _____

17. _____

18. _____

19. _____

20. _____

Worksheet 10-09

I. Fill in the blanks.

____ 1. Ten years is _____.

____ 2. Twenty years is _____.

____ 3. One hundred years is _____.

____ 4. There are _____ days in a year.

____ 5. There are _____ weeks in a year.

____ 6. There are _____ hours in a year.

____ 7. There are _____ months in a year.

____ 8. Three decades is _____ than a century.

____ 9. Thirteen decades is _____ than a century.

____10. Ten centuries is _____ as a millennium.

a. eight thousand, seven hundred and sixty

b. twelve

c. two decades

d. the same

e. one decade

f. more

g. one century

h. three hundred and sixty-five

i. less

j. fifty-two

II. Label each picture with a complete sentence.

11 12  13  14  15

16 17 18 19 20

11. _____

12. _____

13. _____

14. _____

15. _____

16. _____

17. _____

18. _____

19. _____

20. _____

Worksheet 10-10

I. Unscramble the words to make a sentence.

1. is this hello Tina _____

2. I yes but money need _____

3. you my friend met have _____

4. Ralph woman the into bumps _____

5. Jonathan Robert hands shaking are and _____

6. George magazine that give please me _____

7. cannot where see going is Ralph he _____

8. is going make to a call Thomas phone _____

9. right writing down I now am it _____

10. me me you time tell could excuse the _____

II. Write three sentences to finish each conversation.

11. Hello, Donna!

_____

_____

_____

12. Excuse me, could you tell me the time?

_____

_____

_____

13. Hello, Robert, nice to meet you.

_____

_____

_____

14. Hello, this is Helen.

_____

_____

_____

15. Can you go to the store now?

_____

_____

_____

Extra Practice Unit 10

Write a letter in response to the letter below.

October 14, 2005

Dear Thomas,

How are you doing? I'm fine. My first month at the university has been great. The class I like the most is my European history class. My French class is good, too.

The worst thing about school is the food. I think that I'm going to have to learn to cook!

Please write back.

Sincerely,

George

Across

4. These socks don't ___.
6. Paris and London are closer ___ than Paris and Madrid.
7. The boy ___ be thrown.
8. A measuring cup is used to measure ___.
10. The man and the woman are kissing each ___.
14. Bob is using a ___ to hang a shirt on the clothesline.
16. Annette is rinsing the ___.
19. Annette is putting the dishes into the ___.
22. He is using a razor. He is ___.
23. These people are waiting in ___ in a grocery store.
24. He is closing the lid of the washing ___.

Down

1. ___ are you?
2. The car is going eighty miles ___ hour.
3. Jane is thinking about writing a ___ to Lucy.
5. Bob is folding the ___ .
9. Jonathan, have you ___ my friend Robert?
11. Jonathan and Robert are shaking ___.
12. They are eating a ___.
13. The boy is using a toothbrush to ___ his teeth.
15. She ___ the stamp.
17. The cloth ___ being torn.
18. The plate ___ been broken.
19. A ___ is used to measure weight.
20. A ___ is used to measure distances between cities.
21. He is not eating a meal; he is eating a ___.

Notes

Notes

I. Answer each question with a complete sentence.

1. Kathy, would you please help me find my keys? _____

2. Have you found the keys yet? _____

3. Could you bring me a glass of soda, please? _____

4. Can I help you? _____

5. Which way is the police station? _____

6. Which way is the public library? _____

7. When is this book due? _____

8. Could you open the door for me, please? _____

9. Would you like orange juice or milk? _____

10. Could you take off this piece of tape? _____

II. Write a two-sentence story about each picture. If you like, you may write what the two people in each picture might be saying.

11	12	13	14	15

11. _____

_____

12. _____

_____

13. _____

_____

14. _____

_____

15. _____

_____

Worksheet 11-02

I. Change the verb from the present tense to the present perfect tense.

See the **Extra Practice** section at the end of the unit for more practice with verb tenses.

Example: The juice is being poured. <u>**The juice has been poured.**</u>

1. The water is being poured. _____
2. She is pouring the water. _____
3. The paper is being cut. _____
4. He is cutting the paper. _____
5. The orange juice is being drunk. _____

II. Change the verb from the present tense to the future tense.

Example: The juice is being poured. <u>**The juice will be poured.**</u>

6. The bricks are being carried up the ladder. _____
7. She is carrying the bricks up the ladder. _____
8. The animal is being ridden. _____
9. He is riding the animal. _____
10. The apple is being eaten. _____

III. Change the verb from the present perfect tense to the future tense.

Example: The juice has been poured. <u>**The juice will be poured.**</u>

11. The boy has thrown the ball. _____
12. The ball has been thrown by the boy. _____
13. The woman has sliced the bread. _____
14. The bread has been sliced by the woman. _____
15. She has hit him with the pillow. _____

IV. Change the verb from the future tense to the present perfect tense.

Example: The juice will be poured. <u>**The juice has been poured.**</u>

16. She will drink the orange juice. _____
17. He will eat the apple. _____
18. Will he eat the apple? _____
19. He will be hit with the pillow. _____
20. Will he be hit with the pillow? _____

Verb Tenses in Passive Voice: Present, Future and Present Perfect   **ENGLISH**

I. Label each picture with a complete sentence.

1   2   3   4   5

6   7   8   9   10

1. _____

2. _____

3. _____

4. _____

5. _____

6. _____

7. _____

8. _____

9. _____

10. _____

II. Cross out the word that does not belong.

11. tying, zipping, buttoning, parade

12. uniform, space, wedding dress, business suit

13. traditional, modern, tying, new

14. Japanese, Greek, Arabian, Atlantic

15. buttoning, formally, differently, informally

III. Fill in the blanks.

___16. He is tying _____.   a. military

___17. He is buttoning _____.   b. suit

___18. She is wearing a business _____.   c. wedding

___19. She is wearing a _____ dress.   d. his shoe

___20. He is wearing a _____ uniform.   e. his coat

Worksheet 11-04

I. Label each picture with a complete sentence.

| 1 | 2 | 3 | 4 | 5 |

| 6 | 7 | 8 | 9 | 10 |

1. _____
2. _____
3. _____
4. _____
5. _____
6. _____
7. _____
8. _____
9. _____
10. _____

II. Unscramble the words to make a sentence.

11. blinking is he _____

12. is his nose scratching he _____

13. his arm she is punching _____

14. rubbing forehead is his he _____

15. she his squeezing is hand _____

16. arms straight legs bent are are his his and _____

17. her his around are waist arms _____

18. the against shelves leaning he is _____

19. he beside is shelves standing the _____

20. the the and woman their man arms have linked _____

Gestures, Postures and Physical Interactions   **ENGLISH**

Worksheet 11-05

I. Fill in each blank with an appropriate question.

1. _____ No, she is leaving the building.

2. _____ No, he is entering the building.

3. _____ It is too cold outside of the house.

4. _____ She is returning to the house to get her briefcase.

5. _____ Gary is opening the trunk.

6. _____ Nancy is closing and locking the front door.

7. _____ A baseball will not return when it is thrown.

8. _____ An egg will not return when it is dropped.

9. _____ A boomerang does.

10. _____ A yo-yo does.

II. Label each picture with a complete sentence.

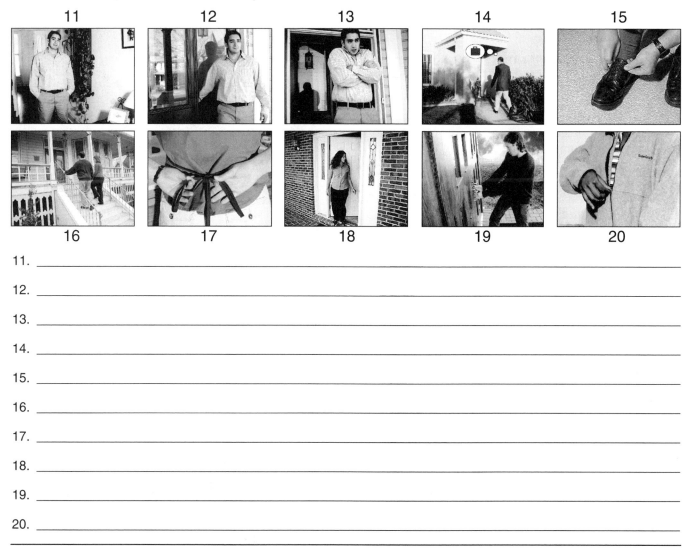

11. _____

12. _____

13. _____

14. _____

15. _____

16. _____

17. _____

18. _____

19. _____

20. _____

Worksheet 11-06

I. Write an "S" next to each statement and a "Q" next to each question.

Examples: __S__ The boy is drinking.

  __Q__ Is the boy drinking?

____ 1. Is he walking?

____ 2. Are they jumping?

____ 3. Carol is running.

____ 4. Where are we?

____ 5. I don't know.

II. Change each question into a statement.

Example: **Is the girl jumping?**   __The girl is jumping.__

6. Is someone walking? _____

7. Is the boy alone, and is he lying down? _____

8. Is the animal standing in a hole in the ground? _____

9. Are the man's arms crossed? _____

10. Are the man's hands on his hips? _____

III. Change each statement into a question.

Example: **The men are riding their horses.**   __Are the men riding their horses?__

11. Everyone is standing. _____

12. The boy is sitting, and the dog is lying down. _____

13. The boy is lying on his back. _____

14. The clowns are stretching. _____

15. The man's arms are stretched out. _____

IV. Add the words to the sentences. When you write the new sentences, you may have to add or change other words.

Examples: **The girl is stretching.** Add: **boy**   __The girl and the boy are stretching.__

  The man is kneeling. Add: **over there**   __The man is kneeling over there.__

16. The man is kneeling. **Add:** young _____

17. The animal is standing. **Add:** in a hole _____

18. The girl is standing. **Add:** boy _____

19. The clown is sitting. **Add:** on the donkey _____

20. She is sitting down. **Add:** shaking hands _____

Worksheet 11-07

I. Answer each question with a complete sentence.

1. Are the cars going uphill? _____

2. Are the cars upside down? _____

3. For a driver, what color of light means "stop"? _____

4. For a driver, what color of light means "go"? _____

5. Where can people buy gas? _____

6. Could you tell me where there is a gas station? _____

7. What kind of car do policemen drive? _____

8. What is the man riding? _____

9. What does "pedestrian" mean? _____

10. What kind of sign tells people how fast they may drive? _____

II. Label each picture with a complete sentence.

11	12	13	14	15

16	17	18	19	20

11. _____

12. _____

13. _____

14. _____

15. _____

16. _____

17. _____

18. _____

19. _____

20. _____

Worksheet 11-08

I. Answer each question with a complete sentence.

1. She looks surprised, doesn't she? _____

2. Did he leave the refrigerator door open? _____

3. He will turn the card over, won't he? _____

4. Is that airplane a jet? _____

5. Did he drop the chair? _____

6. Is summer over yet? _____

7. He cut the bread, didn't he? _____

8. Will he open the door? _____

9. Did she open the door? _____

10. Can she open the door? _____

II. Change the verb from the future tense to the past tense.

> See the **Extra Practice** section at the end of the unit for more practice with verb tenses.

Example: He will run.   **He ran.** _____

11. The sun will go down. _____

12. Will he turn the card over? _____

13. These people will be married. _____

14. She will have a child. _____

15. Will this be his house? _____

III. Change the verb from the past tense to the future tense.

Example: He was here.   **He will be here.** _____

16. He left the refrigerator door open. _____

17. She looked happy. _____

18. He dropped the light bulb. _____

19. Summer was over. _____

20. No, it was not. _____

Questions and Answers Using Present, Past and Future Tenses   **ENGLISH**

Worksheet 11-09

I. Change each active sentence into a passive sentence.

Example: He is ripping the shirt.   **The shirt is being ripped by him.** _____

1. She is tearing the piece of paper. _____

2. He is bending the piece of wire. _____

3. She has broken the cup. _____

4. He has burned the toast. _____

5. I spilled it. _____

6. She has bent the fork. _____

7. He is painting the wood. _____

8. She is breaking the light bulb. _____

9. You are tying your shoelaces. _____

10. We are tying our shoelaces. _____

II. Change each passive sentence into an active sentence.

Example: It has been burned by me.   **I have burned it.** _____

11. The cloth has been ripped by you. _____

12. The cloth is being ripped by me. _____

13. The pages of the book have been torn by him. _____

14. The pages of the book are being torn by her. _____

15. This piece of wire has been twisted by the boy. _____

16. The shirt is being ripped by the dog. _____

17. It has been burned by us. _____

18. The juice has been spilled by us. _____

19. It is being stained by the juice. _____

20. The ice has been melted by the fire. _____

I. Match the words.

___ 1. good   a. wrong

___ 2. easy   b. ending

___ 3. starting   c. impossible

___ 4. possible   d. bad

___ 5. right   e. hard

II. Unscramble the words to make a sentence.

6. this floor to is right the the way sweep   _____

7. hammer use way wrong this is the to a   _____

8. water drink starting he the to is   _____

9. has up the he finished going stairs   _____

10. airplane impossible pick this it up is to _____

III. Label each picture with a complete sentence.

11   12   13   14   15

16   17   18   19   20

11. _____

12. _____

13. _____

14. _____

15. _____

16. _____

17. _____

18. _____

19. _____

20. _____

Extra Practice Unit 11

Write an "X" next to every sentence that contains a verb in the present tense.

____ 1. She is pouring the apple juice.

____ 2. The boy will see it.

____ 3. The paper is being cut.

____ 4. The men ran to the house.

____ 5. They are drinking it.

Write an "X" next to every sentence that contains a verb in the present perfect tense.

____ 6. Will he close the door?

____ 7. She threw the ball.

____ 8. Yes, thank you.

____ 9. The man has found his keys.

____10. The door has been opened.

Write an "X" next to every sentence that contains a verb in the past tense.

____11. My name is James.

____12. Were those bicycles?

____13. He looked sad.

____14. The cat will sleep on the bed.

____15. That was his car.

Write an "X" next to every sentence that contains a verb in the future tense.

____16. She will eat the pie.

____17. The woman is giving the boy a guitar.

____18. He has closed the trunk of the car.

____19. They will run soon.

____20. The woman is singing while playing the piano.

Crossword Unit 11

Across

1. I have a piece of ___ stuck to my back.
5. The cars are going around a ___.
6. not messy
7. The picture is ___ down.
9. not possible
14. not easy
15. Has the sun gone down ___?
16. She was hit by a pillow, and she ___ down.
22. The adults are not dressed differently; they are dressed ___.
23. She is ___ her shoelaces.
24. They are not dressed informally; they are dressed ___.

Down

2. The boy is with his friend; he is not ___.
3. The clothing is being packed for a ___.
4. The paper is being ___.
7. The woman is wearing a military ___.
8. not rotten
10. No ___ is standing.
11. The picture is right ___ up.
12. This animal will ___ ridden.
13. He is not leaving the building; he is ___ it.
17. The man is ___ on his back.
18. The man is bending ___.
19. The water ___ not be poured.
20. This airplane is a ___.
21. The man is wearing a business ___.

Notes

Notes

Worksheet 12-01

I. Add the words to the sentences. When you write the new sentences, you may have to add or change other words.

1. This animal is in the water. **Add:** always _____

2. People eat cake. **Add:** some _____

3. People can get cold. **Add:** too _____

4. Which animal swims? **Add:** often _____

5. Fire is cold. **Add:** never _____

6. Horses are this size. **Add:** most _____

7. Dogs are this size. **Add:** a few _____

8. Mammals climb trees. **Add:** sometimes _____

9. These people carry guns. **Add:** seldom _____

10. This man is carrying a gun. **Add:** woman _____

II. Label each picture with a complete sentence.

11. _____

12. _____

13. _____

14. _____

15. _____

16. _____

17. _____

18. _____

19. _____

20. _____

I. Answer each question with a complete sentence.

1. Is the man interested in the book? _____

2. Is the program boring? _____

3. Does the woman have an idea? _____

4. Did the woman have an idea? _____

5. Will the woman have an idea? _____

6. Can the man reach what he wants? _____

7. Do you understand? _____

8. What could you do if you could not lift a box? _____

9. What could you do if you could not reach something? _____

10. What could you do if you did not understand something? _____

II. Write a two-sentence story about each picture.

| 11 | 12 | 13 | 14 | 15 |

11. _____

12. _____

13. _____

14. _____

15. _____

I. Fill in each blank with an appropriate question.

1. _____ Sure, the bank is right there.

2. _____ I would like to withdraw money.

3. _____ The men's room is over there.

4. _____ Here is your passport.

5. _____ A newspaper costs fifty cents.

6. _____ I'll pay with cash.

7. _____ I think we should take this road.

8. _____ Certainly. You are here.

9. _____ Sure. The museum is right here.

10. _____ It could take you from Paris to Venice.

II. Write two sentences to finish each conversation.

11. I would like to deposit some money, please.

_____

_____

12. Can I pay with a check?

_____

_____

13. Oh, no! Where is my passport?

_____

_____

14. I think we should take this road.

_____

_____

15. Excuse me. Do you know where I can exchange money?

_____

_____

I. Label each picture with a complete sentence.

1. _____
2. _____
3. _____
4. _____
5. _____
6. _____
7. _____
8. _____
9. _____
10. _____

II. Unscramble the words to make a sentence.

11. to himself reading is he _____

12. else to is he reading someone _____

13. themselves children the by are _____

14. the are with their parents children _____

15. woman herself weighing the is _____

16. is at the himself man looking _____

17. woman hugging herself is the _____

18. her is the hugging woman _____

19. they are at looking themselves _____

20. at are we them looking _____

Reflexive and Related Verbs   **ENGLISH**

Worksheet 12-05

I. Match the words.

____ 1. cat   a. baa

____ 2. dog   b. bark

____ 3. cow   c. meow

____ 4. sheep   d. moo

II. Fill in the blanks.

____ 5. The man has a low _____.   a. ringing

____ 6. The sound of a whisper is _____.   b. blowing

____ 7. The sound of a shout is _____.   c. soft

____ 8. She is _____ the bell.   d. voice

____ 9. He is _____ the whistle.   e. playing

____ 10. She is _____ the guitar.   f. loud

III. Label each picture with a complete sentence.

11	12	13	14	15

16	17	18	19	20

11. _____

12. _____

13. _____

14. _____

15. _____

16. _____

17. _____

18. _____

19. _____

20. _____

I. Label each picture with a complete sentence.

1 2 3 4 5

6 7 8 9 10

1. _____

2. _____

3. _____

4. _____

5. _____

6. _____

7. _____

8. _____

9. _____

10. _____

II. Write a four-sentence story about the picture. If you like, you may write what the people in the picture might be saying.

_____
_____
_____
_____
_____
_____
_____
_____

Imperatives, Exclamations; Obedience and Disobedience   **ENGLISH**

I. Change every singular word into a plural word. Do not forget to change the verbs, too.

Example: He is slicing an apple.   <u>They are slicing apples.</u>

1. He is chewing.

2. She is swallowing.

3. She is sucking on a bottle.

4. The dog is lapping.

5. He is blowing into a trumpet.

6. You are sucking on a straw.

7. He is licking the ice cream cone.

8. I am sipping.

9. I am not gulping.

10. Her mother is peeling a potato.

II. Label each picture with a complete sentence.

11   12   13   14   15

16   17   18   19   20

11. _____
12. _____
13. _____
14. _____
15. _____
16. _____
17. _____
18. _____
19. _____
20. _____

I. Cross out the word that does not belong.

1. reptile, bicycle, mammal, bird

2. bicycle, car, insect, airplane

3. map, cathedral, skyscraper, fort

4. map, menu, newspaper, furniture

5. Thomas, France, China, Italy

II. Label each picture with a complete sentence.

6	7	8	9	10

6. _____

7. _____

8. _____

9. _____

10. _____

III. Fill in each blank with an appropriate question.

11. _____ She is ten years old.

12. _____ It is about 78 degrees Fahrenheit.

13. _____ It is a reptile.

14. _____ It is a skyscraper.

15. _____ He is reading a magazine.

16. _____ This is office furniture.

17. _____ She is from China.

18. _____ It is in China.

19. _____ It is the woman's horse.

20. _____ I would like the yellow pair.

I. Fill in the blanks.

___ 1. The man can reach the picture _____.		a. drink milk if he had some
___ 2. The man could reach the picture _____.		b. if his eyes were open
___ 3. The woman is eating _____.		c. because she is hungry
___ 4. The woman could eat _____.		d. drive a car if she had one
___ 5. The man can see _____.		e. because he is standing on the chair
___ 6. The man could see _____.		f. if he were standing on the chair
___ 7. The man _____.		g. because his eyes are open
___ 8. The man would _____.		h. will drink milk
___ 9. She will _____.		i. if she had food
___10. She would _____.		j. drive the car

II. Unscramble the words to make a sentence.

11. food she has is eating because the woman _____

12. any she milk drink if she would had _____

13. pen had he he write if a could _____

14. the woman she because coat a is warm has _____

15. boots his worn would had be he dry if feet _____

III. True or False

Example: __T__ **The woman is drinking because she has milk.**

__F__ **The man is drinking because he does not have milk.**

___16. The man can't see because his eyes are open.

___17. She can see because her eyes are not open.

___18. The woman can go fast because she is in a car.

___19. The man can't write because he has a pen.

___20. The woman could eat if she had food.

I. Match the words.

____ 1. reptile   a. frog

____ 2. insect   b. grass

____ 3. amphibian   c. snake

____ 4. mammal   d. butterfly

____ 5. plant   e. dog

II. Fill in the blanks.

____ 6. This reptile eats _____. It is a carnivore.   a. an omnivore

____ 7. This mammal eats meat and plants. It is _____.   b. a herbivore

____ 8. This mammal eats plants. It is _____.   c. a scavenger

____ 9. This bird eats dead animals. It is _____.   d. meat

____10. This _____ animal is a pet.   e. tame

III. Label each picture with a complete sentence.

11	12	13	14	15

16	17	18	19	20

11. _____

12. _____

13. _____

14. _____

15. _____

16. _____

17. _____

18. _____

19. _____

20. _____

Write a letter in response to the letter below.

December 2, 2005

Dear Laura,

Everyone here says hello. Are you enjoying your vacation? Your brother's jealous of you—he's always wanted to go to Texas. I'm sure it's warmer there than it is here. The weatherman said that we're supposed to get even more snow this afternoon.

Send us a postcard when you get a chance.

Love,

Mom

Crossword Unit 12

Across

2. She is ___ the lollipop.
4. The man has a ___ voice, not a high voice.
7. ___ the butter, please.
8. Watch ___! Broken glass!
9. People can get ___ cold.
11. Frogs are ___.
15. The man is washing his ___ face.
16. A ___ horses are this size.
21. The woman is a bank ___.
23. Cats are ___.
24. The sound of a shout is ___.

Down

1. Fish are ___ in the water.
3. I would like to ___ a check.
5. Many birds ___ fly.
6. not interesting
7. This animal eats ___. It is a herbivore.
10. The girl has a ___ voice, not a low voice.
12. I'll ___ with cash.
13. Butterflies are ___.
14. The sound of a whisper is ___.
17. He ___ a question.
18. This bird eats ___ animals; it is a scavenger.
19. not wild
20. He is ringing the ___.
22. The child is sitting on her mother's ___.

Notes

Notes

Worksheet 13-01

I. Fill in the blanks.

____ 1. We can't see the entire vehicle _____.

____ 2. We can't see the boy _____.

____ 3. We can't see the woman's face _____.

____ 4. We can't tell what time it is _____.

____ 5. We can't see _____.

____ 6. We can't tell _____.

____ 7. _____ who this man is.

____ 8. _____ the bottom half of the boy.

____ 9. We can see the man's feet, _____.

____10. We can't see the man's feet, _____.

a. because her back is toward us

b. because he's hiding under a coat

c. We can't see

d. but we can see his head

e. because the clock is too far away

f. because it is covered

g. the man's head or feet

h. and we can see his head

i. We don't know

j. whether this baby is a boy or a girl

II. Label each picture with a complete sentence.

11.
12.
13.
14.
15.
16.
17.
18.
19.
20.

11. _____

12. _____

13. _____

14. _____

15. _____

16. _____

17. _____

18. _____

19. _____

20. _____

Worksheet 13-02

I. Label each picture with a complete sentence.

1 2 3 4 5

6 7 8 9 10

1. _____

2. _____

3. _____

4. _____

5. _____

6. _____

7. _____

8. _____

9. _____

10. _____

II. Unscramble the words to make a sentence.

11. a dragging chair is he

12. are her following they

13. balancing book head he is the on his

14. inside them leading she is

15. anything they are not building

III. True or False

____16. He is tightening the grass.

____17. She is following herself.

____18. She is balancing a pitcher in her head.

____19. She is popping the tie.

____20. It is hard to walk while balancing a pitcher of water.

New Verbs

ENGLISH

Worksheet 13-03

I. Change every plural word into a singular word. Do not forget to change the verbs, too.

Example: These are plants.   <u>This is a plant.</u>_____

1. These are marketplaces.   _____

2. These are department stores.   _____

3. They are buying snacks from the vending machines.   _____

4. These women are buying plants.   _____

5. How much do these cost?   _____

6. These are expensive cars.   _____

7. The men do not own these trains.   _____

8. These bracelets are not worth much.   _____

9. These machines sell soda.   _____

10. These cars are worth a lot of money.   _____

II. Answer each question with a complete sentence.

11. How much does the snack cost?   _____

12. Is someone buying a newspaper in a store?   _____

13. How much does the newspaper cost?   _____

14. What is this woman selling?   _____

15. Is this an expensive car?   _____

16. Is someone buying a snack from the vending machine?   _____

17. Which item costs the most—a car, a T-shirt, or a television?   _____

18. Which item costs the least—a T-shirt, a newspaper, or a television?   _____

19. What costs less than a car, but more than a T-shirt?   _____

20. What costs more than a newspaper, but less than a television?   _____

Worksheet 13-04

I. Label each picture with a complete sentence.

1   2   3   4   5

6   7   8   9   10

1. _____

2. _____

3. _____

4. _____

5. _____

6. _____

7. _____

8. _____

9. _____

10. _____

II. Unscramble the words to make a sentence.

11. she is home eating at   _____

12. snacks these people eating are   _____

13. is out eating he   _____

14. buying bakery bread is in he a   _____

15. these eating people are a restaurant at   _____

16. something is putting a pan she into   _____

17. buy eat to a a is meal this and place   _____

18. getting hair barber is he his cut shop at a   _____

19. this place to to buy food is a a at make home meal   _____

20. shoes shoe trying store is he on a in   _____

Eating In and Eating Out; Food Preparation   **ENGLISH**

I. Fill in the blanks.

_____ 1. He is pushing _____.

_____ 2. She is putting _____.

_____ 3. He is looking _____.

_____ 4. The customer is writing a _____.

_____ 5. The customer is putting a _____ into the cart.

_____ 6. The cashier is ringing up the items on the _____.

_____ 7. The customers _____ out of the store.

_____ 8. The customers _____ at the checkout counter.

_____ 9. She _____ of the car.

_____ 10. He _____ into the car.

a. at some meat

b. check

c. is putting the groceries

d. are carrying the groceries

e. a shopping cart

f. is opening the back door

g. milk into the shopping cart

h. are in line

i. bunch of bananas

j. cash register

II. Label each picture with a complete sentence.

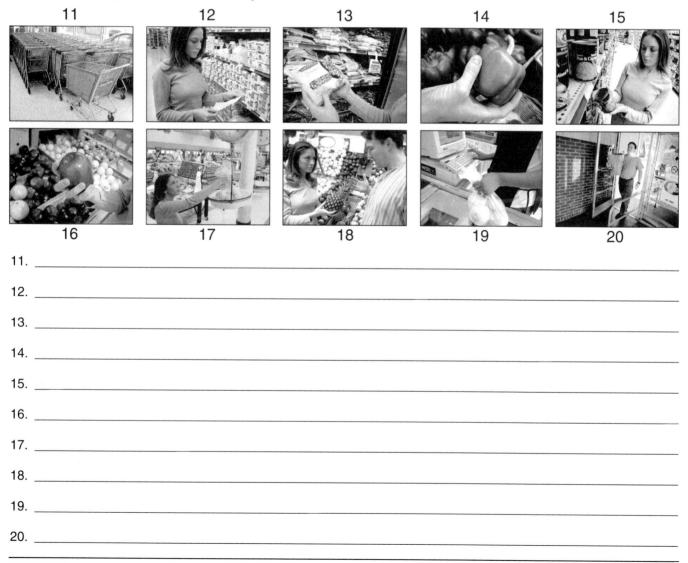

11. _____

12. _____

13. _____

14. _____

15. _____

16. _____

17. _____

18. _____

19. _____

20. _____

Worksheet 13-06

I. Answer each question with a complete sentence.

1. Do these people speak Russian? _____

2. Does this person speak Japanese? _____

3. In this country, do people speak Italian? _____

4. Does this man have a moustache? _____

5. How many balloons are in the sky? _____

6. How many flowers are there? _____

7. Did you understand what I said? _____

8. Do you know the answer to my question? _____

9. Would you repeat that, please? _____

10. Would you say that again? _____

II. Write three sentences to finish each conversation.

11. That banana looks good. Are you hungry?

_____

_____

_____

12. I wish I had a limousine like that.

_____

_____

_____

13. How many bikers are there?

_____

_____

_____

14. That person has a moustache.

_____

_____

_____

15. What did you say?

_____

_____

_____

I. Fill in the blanks.

___ 1. Linda brushes her hair with _____.		a. the window
___ 2. She brushes her teeth with _____.		b. to a tire
___ 3. She _____ her travel bag.		c. a hairbrush
___ 4. She _____ her travel bag into her suitcase.		d. with gasoline
___ 5. She _____ the television.		e. puts
___ 6. She closes _____.		f. a toothbrush
___ 7. She turns off _____.		g. to a gas station
___ 8. She goes _____.		h. closes
___ 9. She adds air _____.		i. turns off
___10. She fills the gas tank _____.		j. the light

II. Using the pictures below, write a story about a person who goes on a trip.

_____

_____

_____

_____

_____

_____

_____

_____

_____

_____

I. Label each picture with a complete sentence.

1	2	3	4	5

6	7	8	9	10

1. _____

2. _____

3. _____

4. _____

5. _____

6. _____

7. _____

8. _____

9. _____

10. _____

II. Write a sentence as directed.

11. Ask for the mail.   _____

12. Ask for the salt.   _____

13. Ask for something a carpenter uses.   _____

14. Ask for something a secretary uses.   _____

15. Ask for something a mechanic uses.   _____

III. Write a sentence to finish each conversation.

16. Pass the salt, please.   _____

17. Hand me the towel, please.   _____

18. Hand me the mail, please.   _____

19. What time is it?   _____

20. Where are my car keys?   _____

Requests for Objects   **ENGLISH**

I. Fill in the blanks.

____ 1. This shirt does not fit the boy. _____   a. fits

____ 2. This shirt fits the boy. _____   b. too cold

____ 3. The key does not _____ the lock.   c. too high

____ 4. The key _____ the lock.   d. It is the right size.

____ 5. The boy can _____ by himself.   e. too much

____ 6. The boy is too small _____ by himself.   f. It is too big.

____ 7. It is _____ to go swimming.   g. fit

____ 8. It is _____ to jump from here.   h. ride the bike

____ 9. There is _____ milk to fill the glass.   i. to ride the bike

____10. There is _____ milk for the glass to hold.   j. not enough

II. Label each picture with a complete sentence.

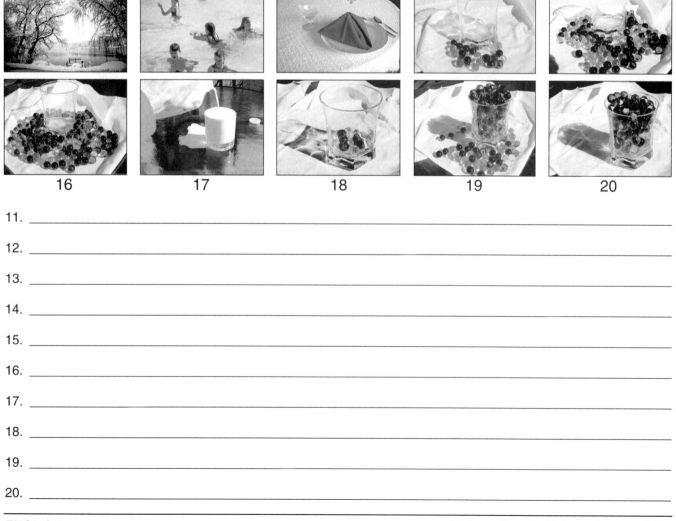

11   12   13   14   15

16   17   18   19   20

11. _____

12. _____

13. _____

14. _____

15. _____

16. _____

17. _____

18. _____

19. _____

20. _____

Worksheet 13-10

I. Change each sentence so that it means the opposite of what it meant before.

Example: This man forgot to buckle his belt.   <u>This man remembered to buckle his belt.</u>

1. This man forgot to tie his shoes.   _____

2. He remembered to comb his hair.   _____

3. She remembered her passport.   _____

4. She forgot her briefcase.   _____

5. He has found his change.   _____

6. She has lost her pen.   _____

7. She has not lost her pen.   _____

8. She has not found her pen.   _____

9. The boy tells the truth.   _____

10. The boy does not lie.   _____

II. Label each picture with a complete sentence.

11 12 13 14 15

16 17 18 19 20

11. _____

12. _____

13. _____

14. _____

15. _____

16. _____

17. _____

18. _____

19. _____

20. _____

Write a letter in response to the letter below.

FLT Express Magazine
122 South Main Street
Harrisonburg, VA 22801
October 30, 2005

Ellen Fairfield
756 Parkwood Drive
Philadelphia, PA 19103

Dear Mrs. Fairfield:

Because we have already received check #1004 on 9/27/05 for $69.00, which extended your subscription through the Summer 2006 issue, we would appreciate receiving your instructions regarding check #1008 for $69.00, which we received on 10/15/05. It can be used to extend your current subscription through the Summer 2008 issue, or, if you prefer, a refund can be issued.

We look forward to hearing from you soon.

Sincerely,

George Martin

George Martin
Circulation Department

Crossword Unit 13

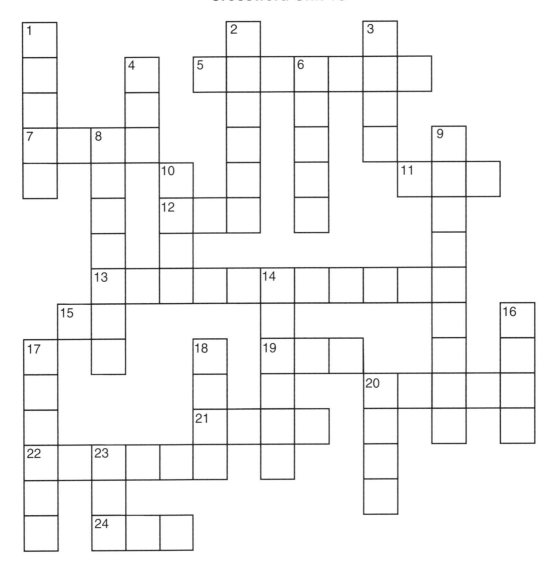

Across

5. She is ___ the table with plates and forks.
7. We can't ___ how many people are in the boat.
11. The mechanic received what he asked ___.
12. He is building something ___ of blocks.
13. not expensive
15. He is counting ___ his fingers.
19. We can see the ___ half of the boy.
20. It costs fifty-three ___.
21. He is putting some milk into the shopping ___.
22. There are not ___ marbles to fill the glass.
24. His shirt is too big; it doesn't ___.

Down

1. This car is ___ a lot of money.
2. I'm just learning English. Would you ___ that slowly?
3. We can ___ see the bottom half of the boy.
4. We can see ___ of the vehicle.
6. She does not lie; she tells the ___.
8. She isn't following them; she is ___ them.
9. He isn't tightening his belt; he is ___ it.
10. A car costs ___ than a newspaper.
14. We can't see the ___ vehicle because it is covered.
16. A magazine costs ___ than a television.
17. He is buying bread at a ___.
18. There is too ___ milk for the glass to hold.
20. The cashier is opening the ___ register.
23. She turns ___ the light.

Notes

Notes

Worksheet 14-01

I. Answer each question with a complete, negative sentence.

Example: Did he pass?   <u>No, he did not pass.</u>

1. Has the girl won? _____

2. Has the man lost the game? _____

3. Has anyone taken the test yet? _____

4. Did she fail the test? _____

5. Has she found her earring? _____

6. Is he using his keys? _____

7. Are the girl's eyes closed? _____

8. Is the boy searching for the girl? _____

9. Does the man know where he is going? _____

10. Am I hiding? _____

II. Label each picture with a complete sentence.

11   12   13   14   15

16   17   18   19   20

11. _____

12. _____

13. _____

14. _____

15. _____

16. _____

17. _____

18. _____

19. _____

20. _____

English   Winning–Losing; Passing–Failing; Hiding, Searching, Finding

I. Match the words.

____ 1. tongue

____ 2. eyes

____ 3. ears

____ 4. nose

____ 5. skin

a. smell

b. hear

c. feel

d. taste

e. see

II. Fill in the blanks.

____ 6. Lemons taste _____.

____ 7. Sugar tastes _____.

____ 8. Salt tastes _____.

____ 9. This person is making a loud sound. _____

____ 10. This person is making a quiet sound. _____

a. sweet

b. He is shouting.

c. sour

d. salty

e. He is whispering.

III. Label each picture with a complete sentence.

11   12   13   14   15

16   17   18   19   20

11. _____

12. _____

13. _____

14. _____

15. _____

16. _____

17. _____

18. _____

19. _____

20. _____

I. Answer each question with a complete sentence.

1. Was this means of transportation more common in the past? _____

2. Was this type of clothing worn long ago? _____

3. Is this a car from the past? _____

4. Was this done in the recent past? _____

5. Is this a structure from a modern civilization? _____

6. Is this a year in the distant future? _____

7. Is this an ancient building? _____

8. Do people wear clothes like this now? _____

9. Is this an old-fashioned camera? _____

10. Is this type of vehicle used today? _____

II. Label each picture with a complete sentence.

11   12   13   14   15

16   17   18   19   20

11. _____

12. _____

13. _____

14. _____

15. _____

16. _____

17. _____

18. _____

19. _____

20. _____

Worksheet 14-04

I. Label each picture with a complete sentence.

1	2	3	4	5

6	7	8	9	10

1. _____
2. _____
3. _____
4. _____
5. _____
6. _____
7. _____
8. _____
9. _____
10. _____

II. Write a five-sentence story about the picture.

_____
_____
_____
_____
_____
_____
_____
_____
_____

Sickness, Health; Health Professionals

I. Answer each question with a complete sentence.

1. Why is she doing her homework? _____

2. Is he eating something he wants to eat? _____

3. Does she have to stay inside? _____

4. Should she have tossed the glass? _____

5. Should he stop pouring when the cup is full? _____

6. Should she have run in the house? _____

7. Does she have to go to bed? _____

8. Should you do that? _____

9. Do I need a chair? _____

10. Which would you rather eat—fruit or a cookie? _____

II. Unscramble the words to make a sentence.

11. rather TV watch I would _____

12. to to go bed has she _____

13. have a may cookie you _____

14. shouldn't the glass toss she _____

15. don't to vacuum want the I floor _____

16. do doing not he is what should he _____

17. to is do she she what doing wants _____

18. she the cup full should pouring stop when is _____

19. he is his he has to doing homework because _____

20. she to cookies eat wants but to has she salad eat _____

Worksheet 14-06

I. Label each picture with a complete sentence.

1   2   3   4   5

6   7   8   9   10

1. _____
2. _____
3. _____
4. _____
5. _____
6. _____
7. _____
8. _____
9. _____
10. _____

II. Fill in each blank with an appropriate question.

11. _____ Clothes are made of cloth.

12. _____ Houses are made of wood.

13. _____ Knives are made of metal.

14. _____ Books are made of paper.

15. _____ Cups are made of glass.

16. _____ Computers are made of plastic and metal.

17. _____ Cars are made of these materials.

18. _____ This material is used to make windows.

19. _____ Cake is made from these ingredients.

20. _____ These tools are used to repair cars.

Materials; Passive Voice; Infinitives   **ENGLISH**

Worksheet 14-07

I. Fill in the blanks.

____ 1. This piece of lumber is _____ horizontal nor vertical.

____ 2. The _____ of the circle is red.

____ 3. This is a _____ angle.

____ 4. The red line does not _____ the angle.

____ 5. This is a _____ star.

____ 6. This is an _____ star.

____ 7. This is the _____ answer to the multiplication problem.

____ 8. Ten _____ of this circle is colored green.

____ 9. More than _____ of the area of this square is colored red.

____10. Twenty-two divided by two is _____ to eleven.

a. correct

b. bisect

c. equal

d. radius

e. neither

f. incomplete

g. one-fourth

h. degree

i. complete

j. percent

II. Label each picture with a complete sentence.

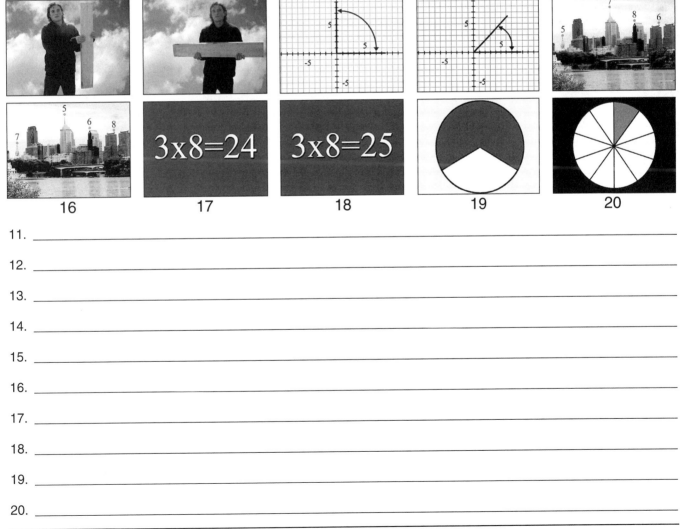

11.   12.   13.   14.   15.

16.   17.   18.   19.   20.

11. _____

12. _____

13. _____

14. _____

15. _____

16. _____

17. _____

18. _____

19. _____

20. _____

I. Answer each question with a complete sentence.

1. When was she born? _____

2. How much does he weigh? _____

3. How tall are you? _____

4. What is the doctor using to check her heartbeat? _____

5. What is the nurse using to draw his blood? _____

II. Using the pictures below, write a story about a person who goes to the doctor.

_____

_____

_____

_____

_____

_____

_____

_____

_____

_____

_____

_____

_____

_____

Worksheet 14-09

I. Fill in the blanks.

____ 1. These three men are _____.

____ 2. Many soldiers together form an _____.

____ 3. Soldiers wear _____ to protect their heads.

____ 4. This castle was built for _____.

____ 5. This wall was built to _____ a country.

____ 6. These men are fighting in a _____.

____ 7. The soldiers are working on the _____.

____ 8. The children are playing with _____ soldiers.

____ 9. The men are fighting with _____.

____ 10. This is a _____ jet.

a. helmets

b. civilian

c. soldiers

d. war

e. protect

f. protection

g. toy

h. army

i. helicopter

j. swords

II. Label each picture with a complete sentence.

11. _____

12. _____

13. _____

14. _____

15. _____

16. _____

17. _____

18. _____

19. _____

20. _____

I. Match the words on the left with the contractions on the right.

_____ 1. has not

_____ 2. cannot

_____ 3. will not

_____ 4. does not

_____ 5. have not

a. won't

b. hasn't

c. haven't

d. can't

e. doesn't

II. Change each sentence so that it includes one or more contractions.

Example: He will not run.   He won't run. _____

6. The girl has not jumped yet. _____

7. The girl has not jumped, and she will not. _____

8. They have not hit the ground yet. _____

9. He does not like the food. _____

10. She cannot reach the box. _____

III. Add the words to the sentences.

11. She hasn't eaten the apple. **Add:** yet _____

12. It is four thirty. **Add:** almost _____

13. He has finished reading the book. **Add:** nearly _____

14. It is one o'clock. **Add:** exactly _____

15. He hasn't fallen off the horse. **Add:** yet _____

IV. Label each picture with a complete sentence.

| 16 | 17 | 18 | 19 | 20 |

16. _____

17. _____

18. _____

19. _____

20. _____

Completed Actions; Approximations; Causation; Actions against Presumption   **ENGLISH**

Extra Practice Unit 14

Pretend that you are going to a new school and have to fill out the following entrance form. Feel free to make up the information that you put on the form.

International Student Entrance Form

Name_____ / _____ Sex: M F
         Last   First   Middle   Preferred First Name

Address_____City_____State_____Zip_____

Phone (_____)_____

Birthdate_____ Last grade or level of school_____

Student lives with: ___both parents ___father ___mother ___other (specify)_____

Father's name_____ Daytime phone_____

Mother's name_____ Daytime phone_____

Guardian (if applicable)_____ Daytime phone_____

Names and current school grades of siblings:

How did you learn to read and speak English? How long have you studied English?

Which of the following statements best describes your English abilities?

1. Cannot read or speak English.
2. Can read but not speak English.
3. Cannot read but can speak English conversationally.
4. Can read and speak some English with assistance.
5. Can read and write English but cannot speak well.
6. Can read and speak English fluently.

What is your TOEFL score? (200–800)_____

List athletic and non-athletic extracurricular participation in your previous school.

List any offices you have held in a club or organization.

List hobbies or interests not mentioned above.

Crossword Unit 14

Across

1. These soldiers are fighting in a ___.
4. Sugar tastes ___.
5. She should do her homework ___ of playing dominoes.
7. Which would you ___ eat—fruit or ice cream?
9. She has not failed the test; she has ___ it.
13. Soup is made from these ___.
16. This is a ninety degree ___.
17. This means of transportation was more common in the ___.
18. The children are playing with ___ soldiers.
19. The woman is dressed like this ___ of the weather.
21. In the past, people ___ in houses like this.
22. The man is dressed in a coat even ___ it is warm.

Down

1. She is watching TV because she ___ to.
2. The man has not eaten the apple ___.
3. Knives are made of ___.
4. not dull
6. He has not won; he has ___.
8. He is doing his homework because he ___ to.
10. I have a stomach ___.
11. She ___ 123 pounds.
12. not correct
14. In ___ of being tall, she can't reach the box.
15. Many soldiers together form an ___.
17. The nurse is giving the patient a ___.
20. This type of vehicle was used long ___.

Notes

Notes

I. Label each picture with a complete sentence.

1   2   3   4   5

6   7   8   9   10

1. _____

2. _____

3. _____

4. _____

5. _____

6. _____

7. _____

8. _____

9. _____

10. _____

II. Answer each question with a complete sentence.

11. Is he crying? _____

12. Is she bored? _____

13. Is he surprised? _____

14. Are they tired? _____

15. Are they angry? _____

16. Why is the man afraid? _____

17. Why is the woman crying? _____

18. Why is the man happy? _____

19. Why is the woman bored? _____

20. How are you doing, Frank? _____

Worksheet 15-02

I. Put the months in order. The first two have been done for you.

1. July   **January** _____

2. September   **February** _____

3. June _____

4. March _____

5. August _____

6. November _____

7. February _____

8. December _____

9. May _____

10. April _____

11. October _____

12. January _____

II. Answer each question with a complete sentence.

13. What is the first day of the week? _____

14. What is the second day of the week? _____

15. What is the third day of the week? _____

16. What is the fourth day of the week? _____

17. What is the fifth day of the week? _____

18. What is the sixth day of the week? _____

19. What is the seventh day of the week? _____

20. What is a weekend? _____

I. Change every singular word into a plural word. Do not forget to change the verbs, too.

1. The boy is hitting the girl with a pillow. _____

2. The woman is spinning a ball. _____

3. The man is turning around. _____

4. He is squeezing the bottle. _____

5. She is breathing out. _____

6. She is wiping the stove with a dishcloth. _____

7. He is shaking a towel. _____

8. She is drying her hair with a towel. _____

9. She is dipping her pencil into the water. _____

10. He is dropping the paintbrush into the paint. _____

II. Label each picture with a complete sentence.

11	12	13	14	15

16	17	18	19	20

11. _____

12. _____

13. _____

14. _____

15. _____

16. _____

17. _____

18. _____

19. _____

20. _____

Worksheet 15-04

I. Match the words.

____ 1. Prince Charles   a. South African

____ 2. Ronald Reagan   b. Russian

____ 3. Mikhail Gorbachev   c. Englishman

____ 4. Nelson Mandela   d. American

____ 5. Australia   a. French

____ 6. Central America   b. English

____ 7. France   c. Spanish

____ 8. India   d. Hindi

II. Cross out the word that does not belong.

9. English, United States, Great Britain, Australia

10. Japanese, English, Russia, Chinese

III. Label each picture with a complete sentence.

11.   12.   13.   14.   15.

16.   17.   18.   19.   20.

11. _____

12. _____

13. _____

14. _____

15. _____

16. _____

17. _____

18. _____

19. _____

20. _____

Ten Nationalities: Persons, Countries, Languages   **ENGLISH**

Worksheet 15-05

I. Label each picture with a complete sentence.

1	2	3	4	5

6	7	8	9	10

1. _____

2. _____

3. _____

4. _____

5. _____

6. _____

7. _____

8. _____

9. _____

10. _____

II. Fill in the blanks.

____11. Someone who teaches in an elementary school is called a _____.

____12. Someone who teaches in a university is called a _____.

____13. Someone who studies in an elementary school is called a _____.

____14. The student is _____ in the notebook.

____15. The student is _____ the notebook into the backpack.

____16. The students are taking an _____.

____17. The students are doing an _____.

____18. The student _____ the exam.

____19. He is _____ hard.

____20. He is _____.

a. writing

b. exam

c. student

d. working

e. teacher

f. experiment

g. relaxing

h. professor

i. putting

j. passed

Worksheet 15-06

I. Label each picture with a complete sentence.

| 1 | 2 | 3 | 4 | 5 |

| 6 | 7 | 8 | 9 | 10 |

1. _____
2. _____
3. _____
4. _____
5. _____
6. _____
7. _____
8. _____
9. _____
10. _____

II. Unscramble the words to make a sentence.

11. behind he her is _____

12. February after is this just date _____

13. the together men pulling are _____

14. the pulling men against other are each _____

15. two the other men are each with talking _____

III. True or False

___16. Wednesday comes just before Thursday.

___17. Wednesday comes just after Sunday.

___18. Saturday is between Friday and Sunday.

___19. February is just before March.

___20. September is just after August.

Before and After in Time, Space, etc.; With and Against; New Prepositions　　**ENGLISH**

I. Fill in the blanks.

___ 1. Americans say 2/1/96 is February first. _____ say it is the second of January.

___ 2. _____ say 1/12/81 is January twelfth. Europeans say it is the first of December.

___ 3. This is the last day of the year in _____ notation.

___ 4. _____ Europeans and Americans say 3/3/98 is the third of March.

___ 5. Americans say 12/11/99 is the _____ of December.

___ 6. Using European _____, 6/1/72 is the sixth of January.

___ 7. What is today's _____?

___ 8. This _____ is March.

___ 9. The day _____ yesterday was Friday.

___10. The day _____ tomorrow will be Saturday.

a. date

b. before

c. notation

d. European

e. Europeans

f. month

g. Both

h. Americans

i. after

j. eleventh

II. Answer each question with a complete sentence.

11. Next month will be July. Which month is it now? _____

12. Last month was October. Which month is it now? _____

13. Next month will be August. Which month is it now? _____

14. In two months it will be April. Which month is it now? _____

15. In two months it will be September. Which month is it now? _____

16. The day after today will be Sunday. Which day is today? _____

17. Tomorrow will be Tuesday. Which day is today? _____

18. Yesterday was Thursday. Which day is today? _____

19. The day before yesterday was Sunday. Which day is today? _____

20. The day after tomorrow will be Wednesday. Which day is today? _____

Worksheet 15-08

I. Fill in the blanks.

____ 1. Someone is _____ a pencil.

____ 2. He is _____ the line with an eraser.

____ 3. She is _____ with a pencil.

____ 4. He is _____ a math problem on paper.

____ 5. Someone is measuring with a _____.

____ 6. He is solving a math problem _____ his head.

____ 7. He is solving a math problem _____ a calculator.

____ 8. Someone is drawing on the _____.

____ 9. She is drawing on a _____ of paper.

____ 10. Someone is drawing with a _____.

a. on

b. writing

c. blackboard

d. erasing

e. piece

f. solving

g. pencil

h. sharpening

i. in

j. ruler

II. Write each math problem in a complete sentence.

Example: 2 + 3 = 5   <u>Two plus three equals five.</u>

11. $4 + 3 = 7$ _____

12. $1 \times 0 = 0$ _____

13. $10 \div 5 = 2$ _____

14. $21 - 13 = 8$ _____

15. $6 + 9 > 14$ _____

16. $12 - 11 < 3$ _____

17. $15 \times 17 > 16$ _____

18. $29 \div 9 \neq 99$ _____

19. $18 + 20 + 22 = 2 \times 30$ _____

20. $50 + 40 - 60 = 80 - 50$ _____

I. Label each picture with a complete sentence.

1	2	3	4	5

6	7	8	9	10

1. _____

2. _____

3. _____

4. _____

5. _____

6. _____

7. _____

8. _____

9. _____

10. _____

II. Fill in the blanks.

___11. The arrow points _____ Africa.

___12. The arrow points _____ from Asia.

___13. This country has one coast. It is on the Mediterranean _____.

___14. This country is an _____.

___15. This country has one coast. It is on the Atlantic _____.

___16. This country has no coast. It is _____.

___17. This country is not an island, but it has a long _____.

___18. This country has _____ on two oceans.

___19. This country is _____ from all other countries by water.

___20. This country _____ only two other countries.

a. landlocked

b. borders

c. Sea

d. coasts

e. away

f. separated

g. toward

h. island

i. Ocean

j. coastline

I. Unscramble the words to make a sentence.

1. to I want cards play _____

2. did laundry he the _____

3. Carol he is toward going _____

4. is not the race to trying he win _____

5. he failed and tried he to the open jar _____

6. from the away is house he going _____

7. they are away her from walking _____

8. this bend trying he is to _____

9. trying the door through is to go he _____

10. succeeded window open tried he he to the and _____

II. Write three sentences to finish each conversation.

11. Did you do the dishes?

_____

_____

_____

12. Did you fold the laundry?

_____

_____

_____

13. Have you done your homework?

_____

_____

_____

14. Which way should we go?

_____

_____

_____

15. I'm bored. What do you want to do?

_____

_____

_____

Effort, Success, Failure; Infinitive Verb Forms   **ENGLISH**

Extra Practice Unit 15

Pretend that you are applying for a job at a restaurant and have to fill out the following job application. Feel free to make up the information that you put on the application.

Restaurant Employment Application

Name_____ Street address_____

First   MI   Last

Apt. no. or box_____City_____State_____Zip_____Tel. no._____

Are you 18 or older? ___Yes ___No   If not, age_____

Availability:

		M	T	W	T	F	S	S
	FROM							
	TO							

Total hours available per week_____Hours available:

Are you legally able to be employed in this country? ___Yes ___No

How did you hear of the job? _____

How far do you live from the restaurant? _____Do you have transportation to work?_____

School Most Recently Attended:

Name_____Location_____Phone_____

Teacher or counselor_____Dept._____Last grade completed_____GPA_____

Graduated? ___Yes ___No   Now enrolled? ___Yes ___No

Sports or activities_____

Most Recent Job:

Company_____Location_____

Phone_____Job_____

Supervisor_____Dates worked: From_____To_____

Salary_____Reason for leaving_____

---

*During the past seven years, have you ever been convicted of a crime, excluding misdemeanors and traffic violations? ___Yes ___No

If yes, describe in full_____

*A conviction will not necessarily bar you from employment.

I CERTIFY THAT THE INFORMATION CONTAINED IN THIS APPLICATION IS CORRECT TO THE BEST OF MY KNOWLEDGE.

Signature_____Date_____

Crossword Unit 15

Across

3. ___ comes just before August.
5. The arrow doesn't point north; it points ___.
8. This person is breathing ___.
9. In France, ___ people speak French.
11. The arrow points ___ from Asia.
12. Today is Wednesday. Yesterday was ___.
13. He tried to open the jar, but he ___.
16. She is ___ the pencil.
18. ___ comes just before Saturday.
20. He is writing ___ Chinese.
21. the third month of the year
22. They are pushing ___ each other.
23. Ten minus two ___ eight.

Down

1. Three ___ two equals five.
2. Tuesday comes just ___ Monday.
4. Today is Sunday. Tomorrow will be ___.
6. She is a citizen ___ Russia.
7. She is drying her hair with a ___.
10. ___ comes just before November.
13. the second month of the year
14. The students are taking an ___.
15. What day is ___?
16. He is ___ a math problem.
17. The arrow points ___.
19. the fourth month of the year

Notes

Notes

I. Label each picture with a complete sentence.

1   2   3   4   5

6   7   8   9   10

1. _____

2. _____

3. _____

4. _____

5. _____

6. _____

7. _____

8. _____

9. _____

10. _____

II. Answer each question with a complete sentence.

11. What time is it?   _____

12. What's the weather like?   _____

13. When do people eat breakfast?   _____

14. When do people eat lunch?   _____

15. When do people eat dinner?   _____

16. When do most people sleep?   _____

17. It's raining outside. What do I need?   _____

18. It's snowing outside. What do I need?   _____

19. It's sunny outside. What do I need?   _____

20. I'm on the moon. What do I need?   _____

I. Fill in each blank with an appropriate question.

1. _____   Let's go to a restaurant.

2. _____   Here is a menu.

3. _____   I recommend the steak.

4. _____   I would like a salad.

5. _____   Here is the salt.

6. _____   I'm sorry. Here's a plate.

7. _____   I'm sorry. Here's a fork.

8. _____   I would like cake for dessert.

9. _____   The women's room is over there.

10. _____   Here is the check.

II. Write two sentences to finish each conversation.

11. I'm hungry.

_____

_____

12. Would you like something to drink to start with?

_____

_____

13. May I take your order?

_____

_____

14. Would you like something for dessert?

_____

_____

15. Waiter, we would like the check, please.

_____

_____

Dining Out; Talking to a Waiter; Modal Verbs   **ENGLISH**

Worksheet 16-03

I. Label each picture with a complete sentence.

1   2   3   4   5

6   7   8   9   10

1. _____

2. _____

3. _____

4. _____

5. _____

6. _____

7. _____

8. _____

9. _____

10. _____

II. Answer each question with a complete sentence.

11. Are these two people friends? _____

12. What did the man give his girlfriend? _____

13. What are the man and woman doing? _____

14. Is the man the woman's husband? _____

15. Does the woman know the man? _____

16. Have they been married for a long time? _____

17. Are they having a picnic? _____

18. Does the mother love her children? _____

19. Do you love me? _____

20. Will you marry me? _____

Worksheet 16-04

I. Add punctuation to each sentence.

Example: She said Thank you James   <u>She said, "Thank you, James."</u>   .

1. Soldiers wear uniforms like these today but they didn't long ago

   _____

2. Soldiers wore these uniforms long ago and they still wear them today

   _____

3. I love you Mommy

   _____

4. Waiter we would like the check please

   _____

5. If it rains we will get wet

   _____

6. The nurse asks Joanna When were you born

   _____

7. I was born on November eleventh 1978

   _____

8. I said That banana looks good I'm hungry

   _____

9. The old green dragon is sleeping

   _____

10. There are many red balloons she said

    _____

II. Fill in the blanks.

____11. Armor was used by knights _____ 1100 and 1500.   a. anymore

____12. Cannons were used _____ 1800.   b. once

____13. Tanks are used _____.   c. long ago

____14. This structure was built thousands of years _____.   d. between

____15. Soldiers wear uniforms like these today, but they didn't _____.   e. Egypt

____16. Soldiers wore these uniforms long ago, but they don't _____.   f. around

____17. Soldiers wore these uniforms long ago, and they _____ wear them today.   g. still

____18. This clothing was _____ worn in Europe.   h. Middle East

____19. This clothing is worn in the _____.   i. ago

____20. This structure is in _____.   j. today

I. Label each picture with a complete sentence.

1	2	3	4	5

6	7	8	9	10

1. _____

2. _____

3. _____

4. _____

5. _____

6. _____

7. _____

8. _____

9. _____

10. _____

II. Write a story about a thief who steals a wallet, is caught by a policeman, and goes to jail.

_____

_____

_____

_____

_____

_____

_____

Worksheet 16-06

I. Fill in the blanks.

___ 1. This is the _____ hand of the clock.

___ 2. This is a _____ clock. It does not have hands.

___ 3. If it is two _____, then this watch must be five minutes fast.

___ 4. People used this to _____ time in the recent past.

___ 5. At this time of day, many people go to bed. This is _____ in the day.

___ 6. The sun is _____ at noon.

___ 7. The sun comes up in the morning. We call this _____.

___ 8. The sun goes down in the evening. We call this _____.

___ 9. Many people eat their breakfast at this time of day. This is _____ in the day.

___10. If it is eleven o'clock, then this watch must be _____.

a. sunset

b. sunrise

c. late

d. second

e. o'clock

f. digital

g. early

h. right

i. tell

j. high

II. Label each picture with a complete sentence.

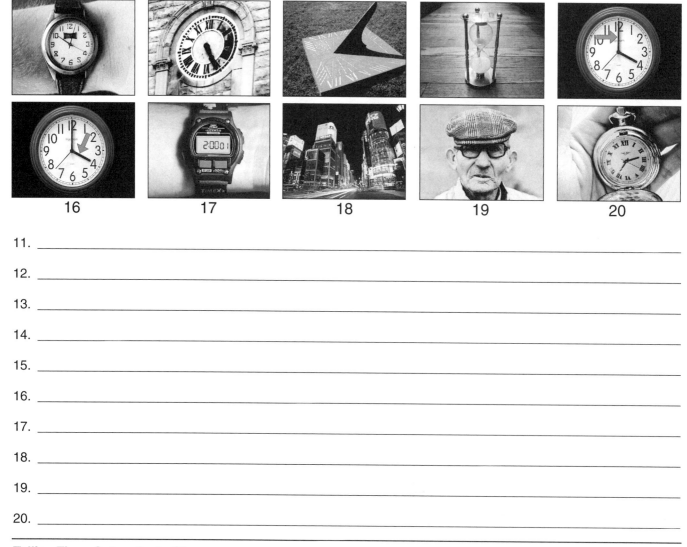

11. _____

12. _____

13. _____

14. _____

15. _____

16. _____

17. _____

18. _____

19. _____

20. _____

Telling Time; Subordinate Clauses   **ENGLISH**

I. Label each picture with a complete sentence.

1   2   3   4   5

6   7   8   9   10

1. _____
2. _____
3. _____
4. _____
5. _____
6. _____
7. _____
8. _____
9. _____
10. _____

II. Unscramble the words to make a sentence.

11. island is this country an   _____

12. Britain Great is this   _____

13. a not is country this   _____

14. was the Empire this French   _____

15. now an country this independent is   _____

16. this independent country long ago time a an was   _____

17. France one at time this ruled country   _____

18. Swahili country in people this speak   _____

19. Britain rule all to used Great countries these of   _____

20. Union countries to part the Soviet these used be of   _____

Worksheet 16-08

I. Match each sentence on the left with a name on the right.

____ 1. This artist was born in 1606 and died in 1669.   a. Columbus

____ 2. This inventor lived from 1847 to 1931.   b. Rembrandt

____ 3. This person was an explorer.   c. Socrates

____ 4. This person was a king.   d. Edison

____ 5. This person was a teacher in Greece.   e. Louis XIV

____ 6. This man wrote poetry.   a. Michelangelo

____ 7. This person was a painter.   b. Alexander the Great

____ 8. This person was a military leader.   c. Gandhi

____ 9. This person ruled Egypt.   d. Homer

____10. This person worked for Indian independence.   e. Tutankhamen

II. True or False

____11. Galileo was a general.

____12. Beethoven was a composer.

____13. Napoleon was the leader of the Catholic Church.

____14. Confucius was a teacher in Greece.

____15. Moses wrote *The Origin of Species*.

____16. Darwin ruled England.

____17. Churchill was a political leader.

____18. Marie Curie was a scientist.

____19. Julius Caesar lived from 1400 to 1468.

____20. Mark Twain was an American author.

Famous Names   **ENGLISH**

Worksheet 16-09

I. Change each sentence so that it means the opposite of what it meant before.

Example: It is possible for him to run. <u>It is impossible for him to run.</u>

1. It is possible for her to read the book. _____

2. It is impossible for him to see. _____

3. She is trying to do something. _____

4. He is not trying to bend it. _____

5. This person will certainly get wet. _____

6. The book will certainly not fall off the table. _____

7. It is likely that she will fall. _____

8. The horse is real. _____

9. It is unlikely that they will get wet. _____

10. This reptile is imaginary. _____

II. Label each picture with a complete sentence.

| 11 | 12 | 13 | 14 | 15 |

| 16 | 17 | 18 | 19 | 20 |

11. _____

12. _____

13. _____

14. _____

15. _____

16. _____

17. _____

18. _____

19. _____

20. _____

Worksheet 16-10

I. Change each sentence so that it includes a contraction.

Example: I am here.   I'm here. _____

1. There is a yellow car.   _____

2. No, I do not like pink cars.   _____

3. No, it is too old.   _____

4. I cannot tell.   _____

5. I prefer canoes because they are smaller.   _____

6. No, I have not.   _____

7. You are right.   _____

8. I would rather go swimming.   _____

9. I like to look at them, but I am afraid to fly.   _____

10. That van does not look nice at all.   _____

II. Write two sentences to finish each conversation.

11. Look at that little yellow car. It's cute. I like it.

_____

_____

12. How about hot air balloons? Would you like to go up in one of them?

_____

_____

13. Where would you rather go—to the beach or to the mountains?

_____

_____

14. Where would you most like to live—in the city, in the country, or in a small town?

_____

_____

15. What is your favorite season?

_____

_____

Describing Objects and Expressing Preferences   **ENGLISH**

Extra Practice Unit 16

Pretend that you are seeing a doctor and have to fill out the following medical history form. Feel free to make up the information that you put on the form.

PLEASE PRINT	MEDICAL HISTORY	PLEASE PRINT

NAME
_____
LAST   FIRST   MI

TYPE OF WORK_____

MARITAL STATUS_____RELIGION_____

EDUCATION (YEARS COMPLETED):

GRADE_____HIGH_____VOCATIONAL_____COLLEGE_____

AGE_____DATE_____

PREVIOUS PHYSICIAN_____

PAST HISTORY (GIVE NAMES AND DATES)

PREVIOUS SURGERY OR FRACTURES	_____
	_____
PREVIOUS HOSPITALIZATIONS , MAJOR ILLNESS, OR INJURY	_____
	_____
	_____
	_____

CHECK IF ANY RELATIVES HAVE HAD

____DIABETES   ____HEART TROUBLE
____HEART ATTACK   ____HIGH BLOOD PRESSURE
____STROKE   ____CANCER
____TUBERCULOSIS   ____ULCERS
____ARTHRITIS   ____OBESITY
____SUICIDE   ____MENTAL ILLNESS
____THYROID TROUBLE   ____OTHER_____

COFFEE: CUPS PER DAY_____   ASPIRIN: TABS PER DAY_____

PRESENT WEIGHT_____   USUAL WEIGHT_____   WEIGHT AT AGE 20_____
WEIGHT CHANGE LAST YEAR: GAINED_____   LOST_____

HEIGHT_____

PLEASE STATE YOUR CHIEF COMPLAINT OR REASON FOR SEEING A DOCTOR.

_____

_____

_____

_____

_____

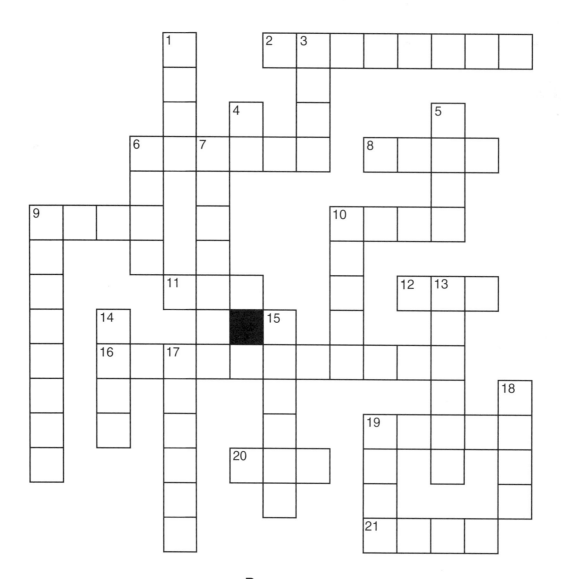

Across

2. The man is ___ another man's wallet.
6. There is a one in four ___ that he will pick up the ten.
8. This clothing is ___ of a Native American.
9. The thief can't steal anything. He is in ___.
10. This woman is the man's ___.
11. They just ___ married.
12. Please come this ___.
16. India was ruled by Great Britain, but now it is ___.
19. The firefighters are using water ___.
20. At ___ time Great Britain ruled India.
21. not imaginary

Down

1. Would you like something to drink to start ___?
3. May I ___ your order?
4. This couple is ___ love.
5. The church service began at ten. We are ___.
6. You wear a scarf when it is ___.
7. Soldiers wore these uniforms long ago, but they don't ___.
9. People in Japan speak ___.
10. This is the biggest country in the ___.
13. Rembrandt was an ___.
14. Louis XIV was a ___.
15. the ___ hand of the clock
17. People eat ___ between 6:00 p.m. and 9:00 p.m.
18. People speak Portuguese in this country because Portugal ___ to rule it.
19. the ___ hand of the clock

Notes

Across

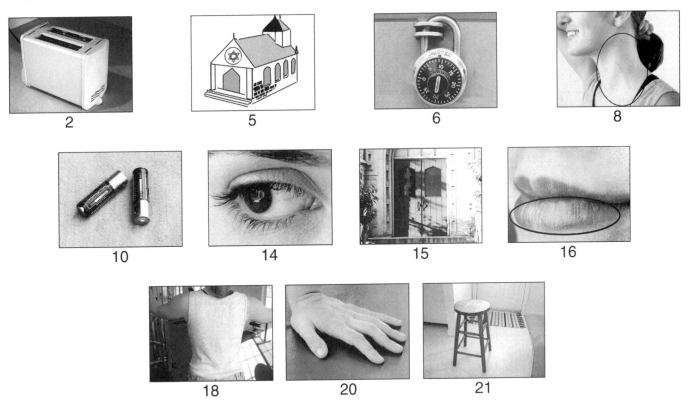

2

5

6

8

10

14

15

16

18

20

21

Down

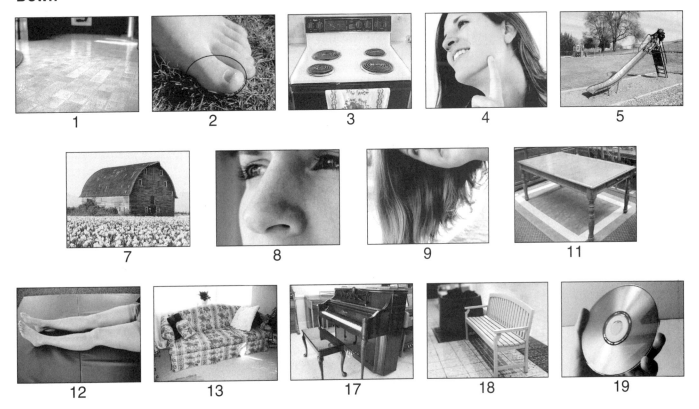

1

2

3

4

5

7

8

9

11

12

13

17

18

19

Across

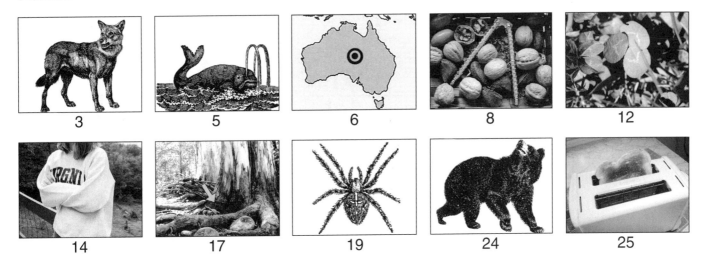

3

5

6

8

12

14

17

19

24

25

Down

1

2

4

7

9

10

11

13

15

16

18

20

21

22

23

Across

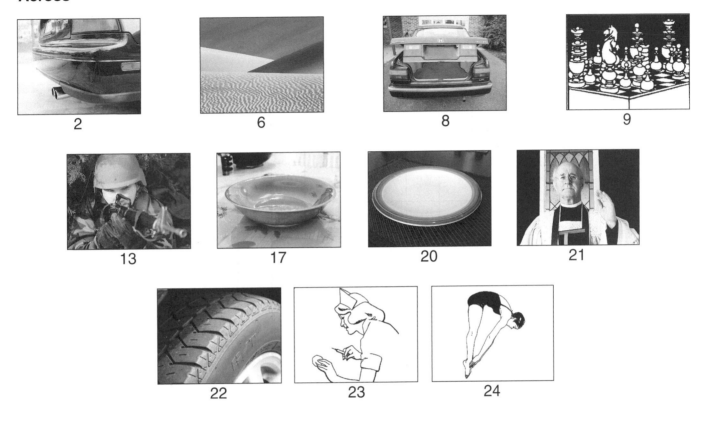

2

6

8

9

13

17

20

21

22

23

24

Down

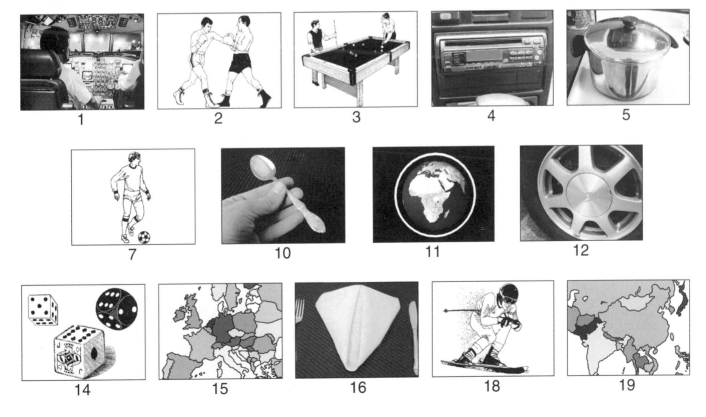

1

2

3

4

5

7

10

11

12

14

15

16

18

19

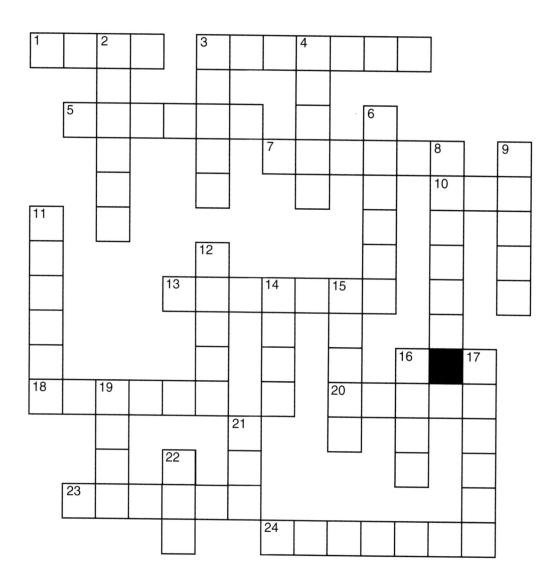

Across

1   3   5   7   10

13   18   20   23   24

Down

2   3   4   6   8

9   11   12   14   15

16   17   19   21   22

Notes